EFFECTIVE PROJECT MANAGEMENT

Lead your team to success
on every project

Written by Nicolas Zinque

Translated by Carly Probert

Coaching 50MINUTES.com

PROJECT MANAGEMENT

- **Problem:** How can I prepare a project and lead it to success?
- **Uses:** Successfully managing personal and professional projects requires great rigour, but also preparation following specific rules.
- **Professional context:** Project management, management, professional development, etc.
- **FAQs:**
  - Does the project manager always have the same responsibilities?
  - How long should I spend in the preparation, implementation and closing phases?
  - What if the financial demands or deadlines are too restrictive?
  - Is it possible to manage several projects at once?
  - What if I replace a project manager at short notice?
  - How can I delegate work?

Whether you desired it or dreaded it, you have just been appointed project manager! First of all, congratulations! Your skills have finally been recognised. You must now prove that this level of trust was well deserved.

But project management is not confined to a title. We are all regularly confronted with this exercise, whether in our personal lives or in our work: from organising holidays to redesigning the garden, all the way through to planning meals. In your career, you have undoubtedly taken part in projects and you think logically that you will be able to rely on your experience.

However, to be an effective project or business manager is no simple feat: it is a challenge which, to be exciting and fulfilling, comes with a high level of pressure. As a leader, you are responsible for the schedule, guaranteeing compliance with deadlines and budgets and leading employees. You will need to report the project development with backers and clients, whatever the result... Therefore, there is a great opportunity for a positive outcome.

This guide is designed for all aspiring project managers, as well as those seeking to improve their skills in this area. It can also be useful for stakeholders in a project: although the responsibility lies with the project manager, their triumph is shared by the whole team. So what are you waiting for? Adopt the right reflexes now!

PLANNED PROJECT MANAGEMENT: THE BASICS

BASIC PRINCIPLES

What is a project?

The answer may seem obvious... but wait! A project is a set of activities (or tasks) conducted to achieve set objectives, using predetermined human, material and financial resources. This definition thus highlights the basic components of a project:

- one or more precise and specific target(s) to be achieved;
- a time schedule to be followed;
- resources that include a budget, a team and the necessary technical means.

This also emphasises its temporary aspect, because although it may last several months or even years, it still has a specific and limited period.

What is project management?

Projects have never been studied and analysed as much as they have in recent years. Indeed, in our society, where businesses are in constant competition, project management (or simply management) must be as accurate as possible to become a market leader. It is almost a scientific approach, involving a set of tools and methods to improve the quality of your project, as well as to optimise production and its chances of success. Specifically, project management allows you to:

- plan the project's implementation and see it through;
- increase performance by being more effective in your organisation and task management;
- assess, anticipate and, in particular, overcome the difficulties and risks that may arise;
- cope with change and unexpected problems;
- manage a team.

The role of the project manager

The leader is both the heart and head of the project. They are not content with being the architect who draws up the plans, they are also the site supervisor leading the work every day and guiding the team. It is not enough for them to give orders; they must also pass the torch to allow the group to take control of the project. Their missions are to:

- conduct the completion of targets respecting the specifications;
- develop and manage the team;
- ensure the daily monitoring of the project and adapt initial plans where necessary;
- deal with the unexpected.

To accomplish these tasks, certain qualities are essential:

- take responsibility;
- have a sense of initiative and make tough decisions;
- surround themselves with the right people;
- manage and motivate the team;

- be a good communicator;
- be able to handle stressful situations;
- anticipate.

If you are not a born leader, you can still acquire these skills in the field:

> "When I started my career 20 years ago, I was unable to act as a leader and I could not pass on my passion. Even worse, my subordinates were not listening. One day, a friend, who is a football coach, asked me to accompany him in the locker room during the game to see how he led his players. I have never regretted saying yes! Following his example, I learned to assert myself, to choose my words carefully, to raise the tone when necessary or be conciliatory!" (Boris, IT project manager)

The three phases of project management

Any good project management is based on three steps:

- the preparation phase, during which you plan the progress of your project;
- the implementation phase, corresponding to the time you spend putting your plan into action;
- the closing phase, which allows you to take stock of your project once it is completed.

It is not recommended to start the implementation of a project without having prepared beforehand. This may seem like an obvious statement, but it is not uncommon to see people diving headfirst into a project, thinking they are saving time. However, do not rely on this preconceived idea, because although you will certainly lose a bit of time in the development of your project, it will allow you to gain more in the long run.

PREPARATION

The preparation phase is often snubbed or shortened. Yet, this is where a fatal error will lead you straight into a brick wall. In fact, this step is crucial because it allows you to:

- define the objective of the project, in line with the business' needs;
- establish a schedule;
- establish the structure and organisation of the project;
- define the budget and the delivery time;
- identify all the inherent participants and train the team.

Define the purpose behind the project and the objectives

Whatever the situation, whether you are the initiator of the project or not, the first question you need to ask is: "What need (within the company) does this project satisfy?". The quality of the project is determined by its ability to meet that need.

the one that best meets the needs of the company. This is why it is important to understand the reasons behind your actions.

The business need therefore determines the project objectives. For example, if the company wishes to establish itself in the smartphone market, the project could produce a model where the cost of production would be between $90 and $100, but features some technologies. A project does not have to be a product, it can also take the form of a service (the staging of a show, improving after-sales services, etc.). A good objective will meet three criteria:

- it is specific;
- it is feasible;
- it is measurable (must be validated by an evaluation).

ADVICE

If you realise, after analysis, that your project does not respond correctly – or at all – to a need for your company, it is imperative to change course from the start. Sometimes it is better to cancel it, rather than risk a disaster.

Make a book of responsibilities

Project management has been officially entrusted to you by assignment. To formalise this need and to ensure that it is understood by all the actors involved in the project, it is necessary to establish specifications. As you carry out dialogue with stakeholders (you and your client), the specifications will develop;

- the target and the description of the expected results;
- how these objectives will be measured;
- an estimated budget and timeframe;
- the constraints related to resources;
- a description of the procedures put in place to achieve the goal.

Therefore, this document describes the project in a broad outline and sets the limits. It represents its foundation: you will flesh out the content in your preparation. All the operations described below are intended to make it happen.

List and organise tasks

Once the book of responsibilities has been written and the assignment has been validated by the customer and your company, your first action is to list the tasks necessary to complete the project. This step allows you, among other things, to assess deadlines and define the profiles you need on your team. This step details your project as much as possible, dividing it into "deliverables".

DID YOU KNOW?

A deliverable is a measurable intermediate result (product, document, etc.) that marks the completion of a part of the project – or the project itself in the case of the final deliverable. Thus, the specifications, models

To plan your project, there are two methods:

- **From general to particular.** Leave your ultimate goal and ask yourself what the key deliverables to achieve are. Then, break them up in the same way, asking yourself which intermediaries are required to achieve them, and so on. The process ends when you can no longer divide them and can accurately estimate the time and resources needed to complete each deliverable. In the case of a big project, it is impossible to carry out this sequence. You will need to delegate some of the work to your team, who will be able to analyse certain tasks and assess their feasibility.
- **From particular to general.** Carry out a brainstorming session to identify all the tasks that must be performed without worrying about any hierarchy. Then group them into well-defined categories.

Simply by listing the tasks, you will already begin to categorise and prioritise. Formalising this ranking as a Work Breakdown Structure (WBS) is the next step. Imagine that you are organising a day of concerts on your campus; you could list the tasks using the following chart, which includes different organisation sections (in a non-exhaustive list):

Organising tasks

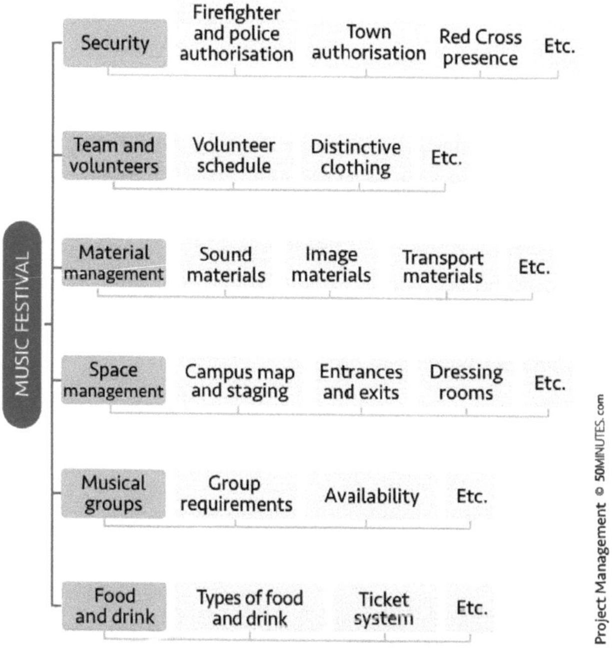

When you make the final chart, you are likely to identify more resources that you will need (What sound material is needed? What image material is needed?). You can also define other categories, including those relating to the budget, schedules, etc. Be sure that all tasks are listed. This method of planning and organising every step of the project is called the '100% Rule'. It comes from the Work Breakdown Structure, a project organisation method developed by the

US Department of Defense in the late 1950s. To summarise simply, this rule means breaking down tasks and making a chart that contains all of the work involved, no more (as this would mean duplication of certain tasks) and no less (as this would mean not all tasks are listed).

Although we have prioritised the project according to the various components of the organisation of such events in our first example, it is also possible to group your activities by departments (of a company), types of costs or by chronological stages (as below), depending on your final goal.

Organising by stages

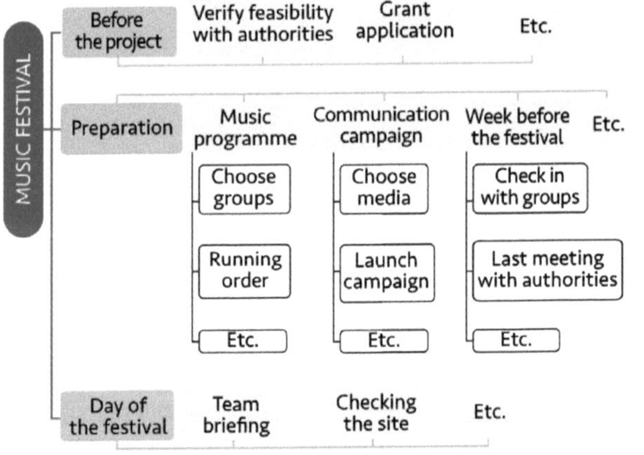

As the chart is visual, it can quickly take up a lot of space. This is why it is sometimes easier to use a simple written list. But remember to give a code number to each task to allow you to locate it easily.

1. Safety
- Permission from firefighters and from police.
- Permission from the city.
- Presence of the Red Cross
  - Possible subcategory
    - Possible sub-subcategory

2. Team and volunteering
- Schedule volunteer jobs
- Distinctive clothing for the team
- Etc.

3. Etc.

Analysing the resources of the project

When approaching the planning of the project, assessing the resources available and the constraints upon you represents a fundamental step. After making your chart(s), ask yourself for each of them:

- What profile and what skills are needed to accomplish this?
- What materials do I need?
- How much time should I spend on this?

These questions will help you to assess the number of people needed, to find competent employees and to estimate the duration of their involvement in your project, as well as giving you an idea of the equipment you will need.

Identify and address the risks

Every project has risks, related to the possibility that an event or an item will interfere in its proper completion. It is therefore essential to anticipate them in order to react quickly if they were ever to materialise.

Imagine that you are planning a boat trip, but the forecast states a 15% risk of rain: do you organise a plan B or do you take a risk and hope for the best? It may be that you are not always lucky. Therefore, ask in advance what could go wrong, then for each task list the obstacles that are most likely to arise. You should also describe the potential impact of these issues on the project (late, over budget, complete cancellation?), and come up with an alternative plan for the worst case scenario.

Indeed, as you cannot protect yourself against all risks, it is essential to classify them according to the probability of occurrence and degree of impact on your project. Remember to assess the probabilities based on your personal experience and/or by consulting experts. Where possible, do not hesitate to rely on facts and figures. Therefore, for a risk that has a 2% chance of materialising and a low impact, it is perhaps not profitable to invest time and money to counter it. Conversely, a highly critical issue that may well arise must be studied carefully. The choice may be more sensitive when facing two extremes, such as a large potential impact with a low probability of happening, or a high potential risk that has little impact.

To prepare a crisis management plan, write down the risks in a table and, for each of them, imagine one or more backup solutions, while evaluating their cost (financial, human and time). Obviously, if the risks are too high and cannot be mitigated, you may need to review the entire project.

EXTRA INFORMATION

If you cannot remove or reduce the risk, you can still buy insurance that will take care of it.

Planning the project

When making your schedule, you will naturally want to reach your goal as quickly as possible... while minimising risk. However, do not rush. Before establishing the overall schedule, you must:

- determine the duration of each task;
- observe how the tasks interact with one another;
- decide the order in which they must be achieved.

To estimate the time needed to complete a task, describe it precisely and identify the factors that can influence it. If you need, for example, a machine to achieve it, this is likely to have a certain production capacity and is perhaps not available at all times. Also, although some of the tasks can be performed simultaneously, others rely on other actions being completed first. You need to understand how they interact to optimise their layout.

To view your activities and the links between them in the best way, you can create a network diagram. For example, say you want to organise a seminar for your company staff. Once the idea has been approved by your boss, you must make preparations for the event:

- Carry out preliminary contacts to ensure their availability;
- Contact potential participants to ensure they are also available;
- Select a date (depending on the results of the first two tasks);
- Book the room (in our example, you have the necessary room in the company building);
- Prepare the organisation of the day:
    - Define the exact content with the speaker;
    - Detail the schedule of the day;
    - Plan meals;
    - Order any necessary material;
    - Send official invitations to the people concerned;
- Arrange the room (in our example, it is possible to do this several days before the event because it is located within the company).

Below, the example is given as a network diagram. Of course, if you need to organise a seminar for your own business, the times may vary according to the constraints (in our case, the project manager feels he needs a week for the entire staff to reply regarding their availability), as well as the potential tasks and their arrangement. Here, the project manager is lucky enough to have an assistant that will help them to accomplish some actions that cannot be undertaken simultaneously.

Network diagram

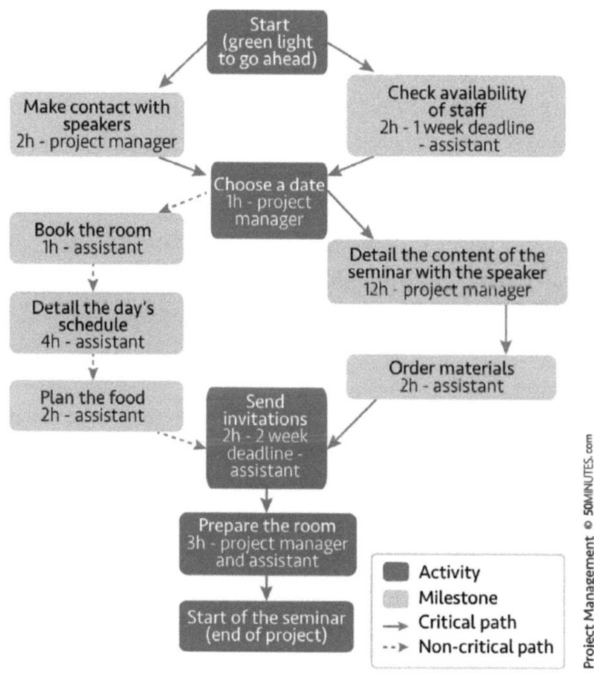

This diagram highlights several important aspects of project planning:

- Some tasks are conditioned by the realisation of others. So long as you have not received a reply regarding the availability of everyone, you cannot book a room (at best, you can pre-book one);
- Other tasks can and should be done in parallel. Relying on his assistant, the project manager may delegate the planning of the day and ordering to them while he focuses on content development with the speaker.
- The critical path, i.e. the longest sequence of activities to be performed between the start and end of the project, which marks the minimum duration of the project, is essential to identify. It therefore follows the so-called critical tasks: any delay on these will impact the deadlines. In our case, we cannot go under 22 hours (if one counts only the duration of the tasks themselves) or three weeks (if we take into account mandatory deadlines: for example, the official invitation must be sent two weeks before the event).
- The margin available for certain activities, which refers to the duration which can be shifted without delaying the end date or the start date for the next task, or the end date of the project itself. For example, the project manager will need to complete 12 hours of work on the content of the seminar, while the assistant only needs to complete 7 (schedule of the day and ordering meals). Therefore, there is a margin of 5 hours;
- Milestones are events that do not necessarily take up time themselves (although this is the case for one of

them in our example). They mark the end of significant milestones in your project.

To complete the schedule, you must set deadlines, i.e. the start and end dates of each activity. To do this, you can use a Gantt chart, which lists the activities, their durations, margins and layout.

Gantt chart

Project: organising a seminar					
Tasks	**Week 1**	**Week 2**	**Week 3**	**Week 4**	**Day of the event**
Find out availability of staff	2h				
Make contact with potential speakers	2h				
Choose a date		1h			
Book the room		1h			
Detail the content of the seminar with the speaker		12h			
Detailed schedule of the day		4h			
Plan food		2h			
Order materials		2h			
Send invitations		2h			
Prepare the room				3h	

Forming a strong team

Through the WBS done beforehand, you can identify the skills necessary to implement your project. For the formation of your team, there are two possibilities: either you are free to hire who you want, or you need to deal with the people you have available.

The first case is ideal, as it allows you to find the right profiles and motivated people, while the second can force you to work with individuals who have no interest in the project. In reality, you will find yourself somewhere in the middle of these two situations.

Either way, take the time to meet with your future team and discuss it with them. Check their skills and motivation, to see if they fit with your project. If you are satisfied, ask them about their availability: will they be working on your project full time? Or are they sharing their working time between other assignments? Find out from when and until when they are available.

IDENTIFY STAKEHOLDERS

It is essential to identify from the outset the different people who have a role to play. Beyond the designer and the project sponsor, identify all stakeholders, both positive and negative, internal or external: customers, potential suppliers, partners, etc. Regularly ensure that they support you and are informed of the progress of the schedule.

Drafting your budget

Establishing your budget means estimating all the costs required for each activity and adding them up. Of course, you will immediately think of the direct costs, such as:

- employee salaries
- expenses (transportation, accommodation, rentals, etc.)
- the purchase of materials (raw materials for making components, technology, etc.).

But, if you want to estimate the actual amount of your project, be sure to consider certain indirect costs, such as:

- the equipment you use in your company (computers)
- heating, electricity, etc.

However, these costs do not always have to be considered, usually because they are not specific to your project, as your company probably already has computers where you work. Contact the financial department of your company to see whether these costs should appear in your budget.

REALISATION

Monitoring the plan

If you have properly prepared your project, your priority is now to ensure that everything goes as planned. For this, you should periodically evaluate your project using:

- regular evaluation meetings (every two weeks maximum) to take stock;

- reports by the members of your team;
- your personal notes.

Additionally, make a quick analysis every week by asking yourself some key questions, then adjust proceedings based on your answers.

- Are the different planned activities being performed?
- Is the budget being respected?
- Are you ahead of time or behind on your schedule?
- Have any of the risks you feared materialised?

Make sure everyone knows the ins and outs of their current task, and that they are carried out according to plan. Be particularly careful when the (expected) end of an activity is approaching and be extra vigilant about your critical path: remember that any delay on this will inevitably delay the whole project!

Following this analysis, either everything will go as planned – in this case, keep it up – or you will notice some straying or even mishaps, in which case you need to get the project back on track.

- Locate the problem: what caused the budget overrun or the delay? What forced you to abandon or replace a task?
- Take corrective action: immediately following this, your goal is not to further penalise your project. However, you cannot always repair the damage. Indeed, if your supplier has delayed the delivery of necessary parts and this affects your critical path, unfortunately you cannot do anything.
- Make sure it does not happen again, acting according to the nature of the problem. If it is a one-off (forgetfulness, inattention, etc.), try to understand why it happened (technical or human error) and take the necessary measures (contact the person, change the equipment, etc.). If it is chronic (a problem in the process), take the time to analyse and come up with a sustainable solution with your team.

But be careful, if you want to make a correction or amendment to the project, tell all your employees and, in particular, consult them beforehand, so that they continue to feel involved!

Team management

Managing your team is paramount to the success of the project. In fact, a bad deal or bad coordination within the team may endanger the completion of various tasks. Therefore, be sure to:

- Guide your team towards the end of the project. Much like the captain of the ship, you must stay on course, against all odds. In the case of a storm, your crew will rely on you.

- Establish and maintain an adequate working environment. You can minimise risks of tension within the team by practicing team building (in conjunction with work meetings, organise one or more small activities that will help employees get to know each other and work together) and ensuring the roles and responsibilities of each are clearly defined and known to all.

> "I worked on a big cultural project, which consisted of creating scenes outside. In this project, the functions and duties of each person were not precisely defined. For example, I was in charge of the general logistics, but I had to regularly contribute to some decorative elements (this is normally the role of the chief designer). On Saturday night, we discovered that we did not have the necessary platforms for the morning scene. Both the decorator and myself assumed that the other one of us was working on them..." (Louis, project manager)

- Define the "rules of life" within your team. How does it function every day? How will meetings take place? Establish a framework and, if possible, include your team in the implementation of procedures.

> "During my studies, I participated in the organisation of a festival of documentary films with other young people. Someone brought us together and suggested we write a charter together. This recapitulated our commitments and defined how to behave in meetings. Being involved in the drafting allowed us to respect it more than if it was a regulation imposed by a third party." (Pierre, head of events)

- Trust them and encourage them to trust you.
- Maintain their motivation. The refrain is familiar: the first few weeks, you will feel able to move mountains, then even if the passion remains, routine sets in and the intensity decreases.

An essential tool: communication

Although it is obvious that you should always have a clear idea of the situation, it must be the same for your team. It is therefore necessary to establish an effective communication system within the group as well as the provision of documentation (reports, etc.) enabling each party to know the project's progress.

The way you communicate depends primarily on the purpose of the message and on the recipient. Both aspects determine the choice of the support and the type of in-

formation transmitted and its confidentiality: although a
supplier must be informed of any changes affecting his job,
he does not need to know your internal problems. Choose
your communication medium depending on the situation:

- **Meetings** bring together all concerned and discuss
  around a table (which may be virtual, referring to video
  conferencing). Do not overlook the account-written
  record of the meeting, which allows for formalising what
  has been said or decided.
- **Emails** are now the most used media, thanks to the
  instantaneous sending and receiving of messages.
  Moreover, they leave a written record which can be effec-
  tively managed using e-mail inboxes.
- **Reports** are used to confirm information and to take
  stock of a specific situation. Their major drawback is that
  they are unilateral. Indeed, the communication flows
  from the reporter to the reader, without the latter being
  able to intervene. This is why they are useful to accom-
  pany verbal explanations (meetings, discussions, etc.).
- **Informal discussions** are spontaneous exchanges of
  information (telephone, around the coffee machine,
  etc.). You must be careful to always confirm officially and
  in writing any key information transmitted in this way
  (including by e-mail).

> "To return to the project that involved creating scenes out-
> doors, a number of pieces of information and changes were
> provided during informal meetings, at which not all leaders
> were present. Moreover, what was said did not always ap-
> pear on the online documentation and the project manager
> was not assured that the information was well received.

> Therefore, it happened that a deputy head learned impor-
> tant changes much later." (Continuation of Louis' testimony)

When you operate your communication choices, weigh up the pros and cons of using oral and written means. Talking in persona allows you to immediately ensure that the message was received, unlike written support. However, as stated by Titus Petronius Niger (Roman writer, AD 14-66) in a speech to the Senate: "Words fly, writings remain". So always keep a written record of informal discussions and meetings.

CLOSING

The delivery

The project ends when the final deliverable is finally delivered to the customer, in accordance with the specifications set. Be sure also to receive a formal written confirmation of the delivery. On your side, you still have to complete the administrative part (report, etc.) and to close the budget. These two aspects will mark the official end of the project. Once the project is completed, it is often tempting to pop the champagne without dwelling on the more tedious tasks at hand: analysis and final evaluations. However, you will gain a lot of knowledge from them for your next challenges!

The final evaluation

The purpose of this phase is to take stock of the entire project. To achieve this, base your evaluation on all your documents:

- Those from the preparatory phases (schedule, accounts,

etc.), which will allow you to compare the final outcome in relation to the basic needs;
- Those from the realisation phases (logbook, regular assessments, reports, etc.), which will help you to understand why the project went well...or not;
- The customer feedback.

From this written evidence, ask yourself the following questions:

- Have all objectives been achieved?
- Was the schedule respected?
- Did the budget remain under control?
- How did I lead my team?
- What unexpected problems arose and how were they managed?

Conduct your analysis and organise meetings (the last meetings) to discuss this.

- Meet with your client to discuss his satisfaction. Also ask them to provide written feedback.
- Arrange a meeting with your team to take stock and conclude the project.
- Summarise your analysis for your senior management.

As you did throughout the project, be sure to validate your findings with all concerned.

PRACTICAL ADVICE

Give your team time to breathe before evaluation...but

no more than two weeks! Beyond that, they may move on and forget information that could be useful to you.

To end on a high note...

Organise a celebratory moment to thank your team and complete the adventure on a positive note. Remember to also invite the people who were present only occasionally. Plan an alternate method of thanks if a party is not possible or if only certain people can make it. There is no need to make it complicated: an e-mail may be enough, but put your heart into it and spend the necessary time on it. Your team deserves a few moments of your time!

TOP TIPS

- **Always keep the end goal in sight.** This may seem obvious, but in the middle of a project lasting several months, which involves dozens of people and countless sub-objectives, it is not uncommon to go astray. Also, never forget that the customer is always right; if the sponsors wish to make changes to the project, it is your duty to listen to them!

- **Take time to break it down.** If you are facing a complex situation or problem, keep a cool head and try to see it more clearly. To do this, break the situation or problem down and adjust the different parts one after the other.

- **There is no need to reinvent the wheel for each project.** Build upon your previous experiences and those of others. Consult colleagues and experts and take note of their advice. However, this does not mean that you can skip the preparation phase. "I've done it once, so I know what to do" is the worst mistake you can make.

- **Anticipate!** Keeping one step ahead is the mark of a great project manager. Although you are unable to escape the unexpected, you can anticipate problems and prepare alternatives. If you cannot anticipate them, resolve difficulties as they arise and identify the causes so that they do not reoccur.

- **It's all about communication.** A carefully planned project may collapse if a change was not communicated to the correct person. Remember this golden rule: any amendment must be the result of consultation with the people concerned. For major changes, the agreement of

the customer is naturally required.
- **Always be aware of the progress of your project,** the project activities already carried out, what is left to do and the state of the budget. To do this, update the balance sheet every week and take note of the elements that cause problems: your first assignment the following week will be to resolve it!
- **Master the tools of a project manager.** For professional projects in business, you might use project manager software, such as Microsoft Project. Learn to control it with ease, as this will save you valuable time. Even for a small project, do not hesitate to take the plunge.

- Collabtive (open source) is a free alternative to Basecamp. It is mostly aimed at SMEs.
- Ganttproject (open source) is a basic program for managing projects, based on the Gantt chart. It is simple to use, but is rather limited.
- Trello is a new software, which is being used by more and more people. Projects are organised in boards with lists of cards, each representing a task. There are free and paid versions.
- Wrike is a very powerful software, which has become one of the market leaders. Users can, among other things, manage and track projects, deadlines and schedules. There are free and paid versions.

- **Organise a "two companies meeting"** to go from the preparation phase to the implementation phase. You are leading the entire course of the project and will ensure that it is clear to everyone.
- **Delegate.** The head of a project plays the role of the conductor. Trust your employees and get them involved in the project as much as possible, as this will strengthen their motivation and efficiency. Also, you cannot be present on all fronts, at the risk of making mistakes.

FAQS

DOES THE PROJECT MANAGER ALWAYS HAVE THE SAME RESPONSIBILITIES?

No, the role of the project manage can vary from case to case and according to the company. Before you embark on a project, it is necessary to precisely define your mission and put it in writing to avoid any ambiguity. Pay particular attention to your responsibilities regarding:

- the objectives
- drafting the budget
- managing the schedule
- freedoms you have in recruiting your team (external/ internal, or mixed)
- the limits of your power, i.e. who you report to.

HOW LONG SHOULD I SPEND IN THE PREPARATION, IMPLEMENTATION AND CLOSING PHASES?

Allow 2/3 for the implementation phase and 1/3 for the preparation and closing phases. A third may seem like a lot, but remember that the days you spend on these two phases, including the preliminary part, are long-term investments.

WHAT IF THE FINANCIAL DEMANDS OR DEADLINES ARE TOO RESTRICTIVE?

Any project can be summarised in a triangle, the three ends of which are cost, time and quality. The ideal situation for project managers is to have unlimited budget and time to obtain the best quality result.

In reality, you will face constraints and you need to prioritise one or two points of the triangle. Imagine that you are imposing a tight budget. After searching through all the possible solutions, it may be that you have no choice but to reduce the size of your team (which will extend the delivery time). If you cannot exceed a certain date, you will need to review and bring your goals down. If you find yourself in this type of situation, inform your superiors, arguing for the solution that you think is the fairest and agree on the final decision. If you feel that the project will not hold up, you can also decline the job, which is an equally difficult choice.

IS IT POSSIBLE TO MANAGE SEVERAL PROJECTS AT ONCE?

In theory, it is better to concentrate on one project at a time, but real life is often different. Firstly, you may not necessarily have a choice: you may need to juggle several projects for budgetary reasons, organisation, etc. Likewise, some projects may extend over long periods and may have calmer phases, during which you will have some free time. Besides, the most important thing if you manage multiple projects is to establish priorities between and within them.

WHAT IF I REPLACE A PROJECT MANAGER AT SHORT NOTICE?

Sometimes you may be asked to urgently replace someone. In principle, a backup plan is designed to address this problem: the successor is usually either an assistant to the former project manager, or a similarly experienced person who has led other large projects.

If you had no affiliation with the project, you will naturally have to see all the available documents, starting with those from the preparation phase. You will then have to organise a large meeting with all the sub-leaders (or all team members) to introduce yourself, define any new procedures and, above all, to listen to the reports from each department.

HOW CAN I DELEGATE WORK?

Being a good project manager means knowing how to assign certain tasks to your employees, so that you can concentrate on the essentials. To delegate, clearly define the powers you are granting (Are you allowing them to validate orders? If so, within what budget?) and be clear in the definition of the assignment, as well as the deadlines. Finally, empower the person to whom you are delegating: explain to them that you trust them, but you expect total commitment from them in return. Communicate regularly with them to make sure everything is running smoothly.

OVER TO YOU

Before starting the project implementation phase, make sure that all the following items have been acquired.

Project preparation checklist

	✓
Ensuring that everything has been authorised to go ahead • I have identified the need to which my project responds • I have made, along with the manager and the client, a book of tasks and my responsibilities are clearly defined in my mission statement. • I have verified that my vision of the project matches the objectives and values of the company. • I am sure of the feasibility of the project. • I have identified the key players (internal and external) of the project.	
Planning the project • I have broken my project down into deliverables and identified the tasks that need to be accomplished. • I have ordered these tasks in the form of a diagram or list. • I have identified the financial, human and material resources needed. • I have estimated the duration of each activity. • I have defined the interactions between each task. • I have constructed a network diagram and a schedule.	
Forming a team • I have constructed my team, paying particular attention to the skills, motivations and availability of staff. • I have set rules for the internal functioning of my group. • I have involved my team in the project, right from the preparation phase. • I have planned a meeting between my team members in order to promote good relations. • I have clarified the responsibilities of each person and set a hierarchy.	

Project preparation checklist (continued)

	✓
Setting a budget • I have evaluated the cost of each task. • I have accounted for direct and indirect costs. • I have contacted the financial department in my company.	
Anticipating risks • I have identified, listed and ordered the potential risks. • I have prepared a plan for managing these risks.	
Evaluating your project • I have identified how to evaluate each objective. • I have implemented a system of regular evaluation.	
Before launching the realisation phase • I have validated my plans and decisions with all participants in the project (client, manager, team, suppliers, partners). • I have organised a final meeting with my team to recap the development of the project.	

We want to hear from you!
Leave a comment on your online library
and share your favourite books on social media!

FIND OUT MORE

BIBLIOGRAPHY

- Bruce, A. and Langdon, K. (2001) *Développer un projet. 101 trucs et conseils.* Paris: Éditions Mango.
- Davidson, J. (2001) *Vous devez gérer un projet?* Paris: Village Mondial.
- Muller, J-L. (2005) *Management de projet.* Paris: AFNOR.
- Portny, S. and Sage, S. (2011) *La gestion de projet pour les nuls.* Paris: Éditions First.
- Vallet, G. (20120) *Réussir son management de projet.* Paris: Dunod.

ADDITIONAL SOURCES

- Bonnin, P. and Bouzdine-Chameeva, T. (2012) *Gérer un projet efficacement. Les 7 étapes-clés sans difficultés!* Paris: AFNOR.
- Buttric, R. and Chanson, G. (2015) *Gestion de projets. Le guide exhaustif du management de projets.* 5th edition. Paris: Pearson.
- Cambie, F., Impe, M., Luna, E. and Marlier, E. (2007) *Construire...et gérer son projet.* Brussels: STICS.
- Cayatte, R. (2007) *Bâtir une équipe performante et motive.* Paris: Eyrolles- Éditions d'Organisation.
- Drecq, V. (2014) *Pratiques de management de projet. 40 outils et techniques pour prendre la bonne decision.* Paris: Dunod.
- Garel, G. (2011) *Le management de projet.* Paris: La Découverte.

- Gray, C. F. and Larson, E. W. (2014) *Management de projet*. Paris: Dunod.
- Hochet, X. (2008) *Transformer l'entreprise. De la décision à l'action*. Paris: Odile Jacob.
- Mesnards, P. (2007) *Réussir l'analyse des besoins*. Paris: Eyrolles-Éditions d'Organisation.
- Néré, J-J. (2012) *Comment manager un projet?* Paris: Éditions Démos.
- Noce, T. in collaboration with Paradowski, P. and Maccio, C. (2004) *Animer, financer et communiquer votre projet*. Lyon: Chronique sociale.
- Noce, T. and Paradowski, P. (2005) *Élaborer un projet. Guide stratégique*. Lyon: Chronique sociale
- *PMBOK Guide. (2013) Guide du corpus des connaissances en management de projet*. [5th edition]. Project Management Institute: Newton (United States).
- Roy, E. and Vernerey, G. (2010) *La conduite de projets complexes*. Paris: Éditions Maxima.
- Sevin, X. (2015) *De la gestion de portefeuille de projets à la gestion de projets. Du décisionnel à l'opérationnel*. Nantes: Éditions ENI.
- Sotiaux, Y. (2008) *Management d'équipe projet. Le chef de projet, un manager*. Le Mans: Gereso Éditions.

50MINUTES.com

IMPROVE YOUR GENERAL KNOWLEDGE

IN A BLINK OF AN EYE !

www.50minutes.com

www.50minutes.com

Ebook EAN: 9782806279293

Paperback EAN: 9782806284044

Legal Deposit: D/2016/12603/350

Cover: © Primento

Digital conception by Primento, the digital partner of publishers.